J9

CH00339646

4 200 001 814 16

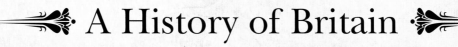

A History of Britain

ROMAN BRITAIN

55 BCE–450 CE

Richard Dargie

W

FRANKLIN WATTS

LONDON•SYDNEY

First published in 2008 by Franklin Watts

© 2008 Arcturus Publishing Limited

Franklin Watts
338 Euston Road
London NW1 3BH

Franklin Watts Australia
Level 17/207 Kent Street, Sydney, NSW 2000

Produced by Arcturus Publishing Limited,
26/27 Bickels Yard, 151–153 Bermondsey Street, London SE1 3HA

Series concept: Alex Woolf
Editor and picture researcher: Patience Coster
Designer: Phipps Design

Picture credits:
akg-images: 12, 16 and cover (Richard Booth), 25.
Corbis: 4 (Bettmann), 6 (Stapleton Collection), 7 (Bettmann), 11 (Hulton-Deutsch Collection), 15 and cover (Adam Woolfitt), 21 (Nik Wheeler), 29 (WildCountry).
Getty Images: 8 (Time & Life Pictures).
Mary Evans Picture Library: 14 (Mary Evans ILN Pictures), 18, 20 (Bill Meadows).
The Art Archive: cover photo, bust of Marcus Aurelius (Museo Capitolino Rome/Alfredo Dagli Orti), 17 (bottom) and cover.
The Bridgeman Art Library: 5, 10 (Stapleton Collection), 22 (British Museum, London, UK), 23 (Dorset County Museum, UK), 26, 27 (Look and Learn).
Topfoto: 19 and cover (AA World Travel Library).

Every attempt has been made to clear copyright. Should there be any inadvertent omission, please apply to the publisher for rectification.

A CIP catalogue record for this book is available from the British Library.

Dewey Decimal Classification Number: 936.2'04

ISBN 978 0 7496 8193 7

Printed in China

Franklin Watts is a division of Hachette Children's Books.

Contents

The Coming of the Legions

For over 350 years, southern Britain was a valuable part of the Roman Empire. The Romans left a strong mark on the land they called Britannia, building roads, forts and settlements that ranged from villa farms in the countryside to rich trading towns like Londinium (London). Their first attempts to conquer Britain were, however, unsuccessful.

Julius Caesar arrives with his troops on the first Roman expedition to Britain. He met with fierce resistance all along the coast.

Why Did the Romans Invade Britain?

In 55 BCE, the Roman leader Julius Caesar invaded Britain. He wanted to punish the Britons for sending help to their allies in Gaul, who had rebelled against Rome. Caesar also believed that Britain was rich in valuable metals such as gold. He wanted that wealth as well as the glory of conquering these mysterious islands on the edge of the known world.

Battle on the Beach

Caesar's invasion fleet arrived at the British coast near Dover. This was no place for a landing, for the cliffs were lined with British warriors who could throw their spears down on the Romans. Caesar sailed northwards, anchoring near the

Timeline

55 BCE	27 August	• Roman invaders land at Deal beach in Kent
	31 August	• Winds in the English Channel scatter the Roman support fleet
	5 Sept	• Caesar returns with his men to Gaul
54 BCE	7 July	• Roman invasion force lands at Sandwich
	8 July	• Romans capture Bigbury hillfort
	15 August	• Caesar learns of a Celtic revolt in Gaul
	3 September	• Caesar retreats again to European mainland

settlement of Deal, but the Britons were waiting there as well. Caesar ordered his reluctant troops on to the beach, but the Britons attacked the heavily armed legionaries as they waded ashore. After fighting hard all day, the Romans only captured a few metres of sand.

Roman Failure

For the Romans, the poor British weather was as much an enemy as the Britons in their war-chariots. The strong Channel winds pushed the supply ships carrying the Roman cavalry all the way back to Gaul. Storms also damaged the ships anchored at Deal. British warriors ambushed Roman troops who had been sent to look for food in the countryside. Without horsemen and supplies, the Romans were pinned to the coast. Caesar decided to retreat to Gaul. The Romans had underestimated the difficulty of invading Britain. But Caesar had learned that southern Britain was very rich in grain, so he was determined to persist with his plan to invade. He spent the winter building up a much larger invasion force of over 30,000 men.

Caesar Returns

The next spring, the Romans landed near Sandwich in Kent. This time they were more successful. Caesar quickly captured the nearby British hillfort at Bigbury, then marched inland, fording the River Thames near London. The British warlord, Cassivellaunus, cleverly avoided battle with the legions, preferring to attack them repeatedly from the thick forest. He also tried to negotiate with the Romans. Caesar was eager to reach a peace. News of unrest in Gaul forced him to abandon his plans to over-winter in Britain. He took hostages, and gained guarantees of peace from the tribal leaders, then sailed back to Gaul with his troops. It would be ninety-seven years before the legions returned.

The second invasion in 54 BCE was more successful, and the Romans soon established a base in Kent.

The Claudian Invasion

In 41 CE the British warlord Caratacus attacked the rich Hampshire lands of his neighbour King Verica, who asked the Romans for help. Verica's plea gave the new Roman emperor, Claudius, a good excuse to invade Britain.

Imperial Triumph

The Roman general, Aulus Plautius, commanded an army of almost 40,000 men when he landed in 43 CE. Two quick victories against British tribes gave Plautius control of most of south-east England. In August, Emperor Claudius marched into Camulodunum (Colchester), the capital of the southern British tribes. Standing at the head of his victorious legions and their war-elephants, Claudius accepted the homage of the local British chieftains.

TI·CLAVDIVS·CÆS·AVG·ROM·IMP·S

In 43 CE, the Emperor Claudius (above) arrived in southern Britain and began to establish Roman control of England.

Roman Progress

Not all British tribes were happy to accept Roman rule. In the south-west, the Second Augusta Legion had the tough job of conquering the hostile Durotriges and Dumnonii tribes, whose lands were filled with menacing hillforts. Some of these forts surrendered after a brief display of Roman military power. The defenders of Hod Hill fort in Dorset laid down their weapons after an opening barrage of Roman *ballista* bolts destroyed their chieftain's homestead. However, archaeological evidence tells us that other British settlements were only captured after a fierce struggle. More than a hundred slaughtered Britons and their shattered weapons were thrown into a pit at Spettisbury Ring in Dorset. Archaeologists digging at Maiden Castle found the backbone of a British warrior pierced by a Roman iron bolt.

The Romans were horrified by the Druid practice of building huge wicker figures which they filled with sacrificial victims before setting them alight.

Resistance to Rome

The Romans also faced tough resistance from Caratacus, who had escaped the fall of Camulodunum. He rode west to Wales to carry on the fight alongside the fierce warriors of the Silures and Ordovices tribes. Caratacus and his allies were only defeated in 51 CE. Betrayed to his enemies, he was dragged through the streets of Rome in chains. With Caratacus a prisoner, resistance to Rome faded away. To ensure peace, the Roman army built forts across the country from the River Humber to the River Severn. By 60 CE, southern Britain was becoming a peaceful part of the Roman Empire.

The Druids

North Wales was the last centre of southern British resistance. The island of Ynys Mon (Anglesey) was a centre of the mysterious Druid cult, which horrified the Romans. In Gaul, Caesar had seen the Druids force their enemies into wicker cages and set them alight. The Roman historian Tacitus accused the Druids of 'staining their altars with the blood of prisoners and consulting their gods by looking at human entrails'. It took the Romans three years, from 66–68 CE, to defeat the Druidic Welsh in Snowdonia and Ynys Mon. The legions slaughtered the Druids and destroyed their sacred places.

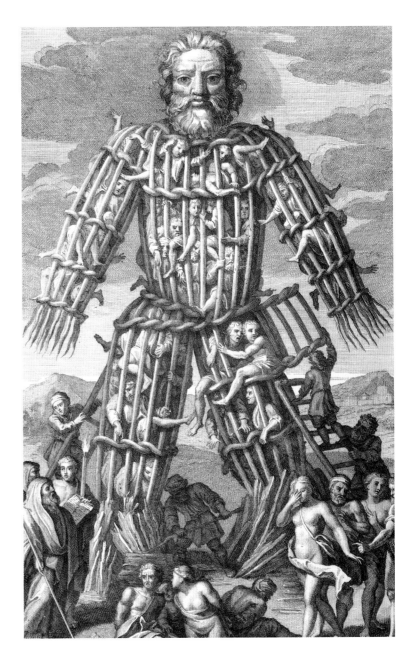

Timeline	
43-47 CE	• Aulus Plautius gains control of southern Britain
44-48	• Romans defeat the hillfort tribes of the south-west
49-51	• Caratacus continues to fight against the Romans
66-68	• Druids of North Wales are defeated

Boudicca's Revolt

In 60 CE, the British warrior queen, Boudicca, led her people in a rebellion against the Romans. While the Roman army was fighting in distant North Wales, Boudicca and the Iceni tribe of East Anglia attacked the towns where the Romans lived.

The Spark of Rebellion

In 60 CE, the Iceni king, Prasutagus, died. He had hoped that his widow, Boudicca, would rule after him, but the Romans wanted his wealthy kingdom for themselves. The Roman officials sent to take over the Iceni lands in East Anglia were brutal and greedy. When they treated Boudicca and her daughters badly, the Iceni revolted. Other tribes, such as the powerful Trinovantes, soon joined them on the warpath.

Massacre in East Anglia

Raising a massive band of warriors, Boudicca attacked the Roman town of Camulodunum. The town had a guard of only 200 troops and was soon burned to the ground. The Iceni butchered the Roman soldiers without mercy. Roman reinforcements sent to help Camulodunum were ambushed, with the loss of 2,000 legionaries. News of the Iceni victory swept across Britain.

The warrior queen, Boudicca, and her army showed no mercy to the people of the town of Camulodunum, a settlement for ex-Roman legionaries and their families.

Some of the myths surrounding Boudicca describe her as a hardened warrior. Others show her as a beautiful young woman who inspired love and devotion in the hearts of her followers.

The Attack on Londinium

Hearing of the revolt, the Roman general Paulinus set out at speed from Wales for the main town of Londinium. Once there, however, Paulinus realized he did not have enough troops to defend the town from the Iceni and that he would have to sacrifice it to gain time. The Iceni brutally attacked Londinium and burned it to the ground. The town of Verulamium (St Albans) suffered the same horrible fate. During the revolt, over 70,000 people were massacred. The Romans were especially shocked by the news that the Iceni had skewered many of their victims on wooden stakes.

The Death of Boudicca

Gathering every available soldier, Paulinus met the Iceni in battle near Towcester, to the north of Londinium. Although heavily outnumbered, the Roman troops were disciplined and won a decisive victory. The Iceni warriors were trapped and slaughtered, and Boudicca killed herself by drinking poison to avoid humiliation and slavery in Rome. With the revolt over, the Romans built forts on the Iceni lands to keep order there. But they also realized that they would have to win the British tribes over to their side by letting them share in the benefits of the Roman way of life.

The Warrior Queen

According to the Roman historian, Dio Cassius, Boudicca was tall, of terrifying appearance, with a fierce look in her eyes and a harsh tone in her voice. More flatteringly, he also described Boudicca as having a 'great mass of tawny hair falling to her hips, a golden necklace around her neck...' and 'wearing a tunic of many colours beneath a thick mantle fastened with a brooch'.

The Conquest of Britannia

After the defeat of Boudicca, southern Britain was brought under direct Roman control. The Roman army there was strengthened with new legions. The trading port of London soon rose from its ashes to become an important centre of Roman government.

Emperor Vespasian (below) wanted to conquer the rebellious tribes of west and northern Britain and bring the entire British Isles under Roman control.

Trouble in the North

The powerful kingdom of the Brigantes stretched across northern England, from the Irish Sea to the North Sea. For many years Cartimandua, the queen of the Brigantes, had been a loyal ally of the Romans who had helped them to keep the peace. But in 68 CE Cartimandua was suddenly replaced by warlike nobles who hated the Romans. The Romans realized that to be sure of peace in Britain they would have to conquer all the peoples living there.

The Roman Advance

The new Roman emperor, Vespasian, believed that the wild, independent tribes of western and northern Britain had to be tamed and forced to accept Roman power. He quickly strengthened the legions in Britain. A large new army base was built at Eboracum (York). The Brigantes were a tough northern people, led by a fierce warrior elite.

Timeline

Early 60s CE	• Romans conquer the Dumnonii lands in the west
70 CE	• Vespasian begins the complete conquest of Britannia
71-73	• Brigantes are defeated in a series of battles and sieges
73	• Stanwick hillfort is captured
74-77	• In Wales, the Silures and Ordovices are brought under control
78	• Romans build forts throughout Wales
78	• Agricola completes the conquest of southern Britain

Nevertheless, they were brought under control by 73 CE, and made their last stand as a free people at the vast hillfort of Stanwick, near Scotch Corner. After defeating the Brigantes, the Roman legions pushed northwards towards Carlisle.

The Conquest of Wales

The Second Augusta Legion was based at a huge fortress at Caerleon in Wales, near the mouth of the River Usk. The legion's job was to keep an eye on the restless Welsh tribes, the Silures and Ordovices. By 75 CE, new forts at Carmarthen, Neath and Cardiff had given the Romans control of the valleys that led in to the tribal homelands. The Silurian warband was crushed in battle, and dozens of small forts and towers were built to control their territory. Futher north, the Ordovices were defeated and the Romans built a new *castra*, or army base at Deva (Chester) to make sure they behaved in the future. A new Roman governor, Julius Agricola, was ordered to defeat the tribes of North Wales. In 78 CE he captured their last stronghold on Ynys Mon in a surprise attack, by forcing his cavalry troops to swim across the narrow straits (sea channel) with their horses, rather than wait to cross by ship.

Britannia at Peace

By 78 CE, almost all the land that is now Wales and England was securely under Roman control. In the south and east, Roman ways of life were already taking hold strongly. In the north and west, the tribes that opposed Rome had been crushed and were kept in line by an extensive system of forts.

Julius Agricola triumphed at the battle of Ynys Mon, crushing Welsh opposition to Roman rule.

Caledonia – the Edge of Empire

Governor Agricola campaigned in Scotland between 79 and 84 CE. In southern Scotland, the tribes accepted Roman rule, but the northern tribes remained hostile. The Forth-Clyde line – from the Firth of Clyde in the west to the Firth of Forth in the east – marked the frontier between peaceful Britannia and untamed Caledonia beyond.

The historian Gaius Cornelius Tacitus (c.56–c.117 CE) documented the Roman campaigns in the north of Britain.

The Unknown Land

By 80 CE, several Roman ships had sailed around Britain. The historian Tacitus accompanied the legions in Scotland in 79 CE. He described the northern tribes as 'dwelling at the utmost end of the earth... there is no-one beyond, only waves and rocks.'

The Southern Tribes

The rolling hills of southern Scotland were no barrier against Agricola's legions. The Votadini tribe quickly made peace and began to trade with the invaders. Many Roman goods have been found at their hillfort of Traprain Law in East Lothian. The Selgovae, based at the Eildon Hills near Melrose, were more reluctant to accept Roman order but were surrounded by a network of Roman forts. In the south-west, the warlike Novantae were only brought under control in 82 CE.

The Lost Land of Hibernia

From southern Scotland, Agricola could see Ireland (the Romans called this distant, misty land 'Hibernia'). He made friends with an Irish prince in case he needed an excuse to invade there. But Emperor Domitian told Agricola to complete the conquest of Caledonia first, so the invasion of Ireland was postponed.

Into the Highlands

In northern Scotland, the wild landscape made invasion difficult. Also, the red-haired, long-limbed Caledonians were fiercer than the southern Britons. Agricola marched carefully along the eastern coast, keeping in touch with his fleet. One by one, the Highland glens were blocked with forts and a major fortress was begun at Inchtuthill in Strathmore. In all, Agricola built sixty forts and 2,000 km (1,300 miles) of road in Scotland.

Down From the Mountain

In 84 CE more than 30,000 Caledonian warriors massed for battle under a chieftain called Calgacus. While the Caledonians stayed on the slopes of a mountain known as Mons Graupius, the Romans made little headway. However, when the tribesmen ran down on to flatter ground they were killed in their thousands by the disciplined legionaries. Despite this, the Roman victory meant nothing, for the tribes did not submit to Rome but simply melted away into the hills to wage war another day.

Antonine's Wall

The last Roman invasion into Scotland was made in the 140s, when Antoninus Pius built a wall of turf blocks and timber spikes from the Forth to the Clyde. He hoped to protect allies like the Votadini and make it easier to police the restless Selgovae. A force of 7,000 men guarded the wall until 169 CE, when plague and disorder throughout the Roman Empire forced the Romans to retreat.

Timeline

79 CE	• Agricola invades southern Scotland
80	• Roman forts built along Forth-Clyde line
82	• Tribes of south-west Scotland are subdued
83	• Roman troops march into northern Scotland
84	• Battle at Mons Graupius
140	• Antonine's Wall built from Forth to Clyde
169	• Antonine's Wall is abandoned

The battle of Mons Graupius ended in the slaughter of thousands of Caledonian warriors and victory for the Romans.

122 CE

Hadrian's Wall

Emperor Hadrian wanted to strengthen the defences of the Roman Empire. During a visit to Britain in 122 CE, Hadrian decided to build a wall across the country 'to separate barbarians and Romans'. Hadrian's Wall was the largest symbol of Roman power in Britain.

Why Was the Wall Built?
Hadrian's Wall was built so that Roman troops stationed there could watch and control the traders moving through northern Britannia. It also prevented surprise attacks and stopped the hostile Selgovae linking up with the warlike Brigantes in northern England. The wall was protected by a series of forts and a deep ditch on its southern side. Hadrian knew that building and guarding the wall would also keep the army busy in times of peace.

Murder Mystery on the Wall
Settlements soon grew up around the wall. Local merchants provided the army with fresh supplies to add to the preserved foods sent from Europe. In the 20th century, at a settlement near Housesteads, archaeologists discovered two skeletons in the ruins of a house. They had been murdered with a knife and their bodies hidden away beneath the floorboards. Perhaps they were the victims of a drunken brawl in one of the gambling dens that sprang up along the wild frontier of Britannia.

The Emperor Hadrian supervised the building of the wall. Observation turrets were placed at regular intervals and sixteen large forts provided housing for Roman legionaries.

What Happened to the Wall?

Archaeologists think that there were long periods of peace on Hadrian's Wall and only a few brief periods of violence. Trouble usually broke out when troops from the wall were sent to help elsewhere in the empire. In 367 CE, the northern Picts spotted that the wall garrison was weak and launched a massive attack on northern Britannia. After 402 CE, payments from Rome to the few loyal troops who were left on the wall came to an end. The soldiers who served on the wall probably stayed on in northern England where they had their homes and families. Over time, the wall and its settlements faded into the landscape and the purpose of Hadrian's great work was forgotten.

Hadrian's Wall ran across the open country of northern England. For the Roman soldiers building it, the wall must have seemed a lonely outpost at the farthest edge of the world.

Wall Facts and Figures

Hadrian's Wall ran for 117 km (73 miles) from Wallsend in the east to the Solway Firth in the west. There was a small fort every 1,481 metres (1,620 yards), a Roman mile. In total, there were eighty of these forts or mile-castles. Observation towers stood at intervals of 494 m (540 yards). Sixteen larger forts were built to house garrisons of 500 men. Most of the wall was 6 m (20 ft) high and 3.5 m (12 ft) wide. Begun in 122 CE, the wall was completed in under five years, but an extra 32 km (20 miles) of defences along the Cumbrian coast kept the legionary builders busy for more than a decade. Once finished, the wall was garrisoned by over 10,000 men, most of them auxiliary (support) troops.

The Romanization of Britain

Southern Britons quickly adapted to the Roman way of life. Many were employed in the running of Britannia and were rewarded with luxuries brought from distant parts of the empire.

Jobs for the British

Throughout the empire, the Romans encouraged local leaders to enforce the law, collect taxes and settle disputes. So the daily running of Britannia was largely in the hands of local British nobles. They served as members of the *civitates*, or councils, and stood for election as magistrates. Tacitus noted that they quickly adopted Roman ways, wearing the Roman cloak, or *toga*, when on official business and making sure their sons mastered the Roman language of Latin. Many ordinary Britons served in the imperial army, encouraged to do so by the promise of full Roman citizenship after twenty-five years in the ranks.

The mosaic floor at Fishbourne Palace in Sussex is believed to have been laid in the 1st century. It features Cupid, the Roman god of love, riding on the back of a dolphin.

Sulis-Minerva was worshipped in Roman Britain as the goddess of medicine, poetry, wisdom, art and music.

Roman-British Gods

The Romans expected the British to honour their gods. Temples to Jove, Juno and Minerva were built in larger towns such as St Albans. At Colchester, annual games and festivals were held to celebrate the spirit of the emperor. However, the most popular gods reveal a mixture of British and Roman beliefs. The Celtic and Roman goddesses of healing merged into Sulis-Minerva, and were worshipped at Bath. British troops in the Roman army prayed to Mars-Teutates, the god of war. In later centuries, Roman traders brought gods from distant lands to British shores, including the Phoenician Astarte, the Persian Mithras-Sol, and the Palestinian cult of Christ.

Spreading Wealth

Money soon became part of daily life in Roman Britain. The growth of trade created a new class of clerks, merchants, money lenders and tax collectors. Goods from all ends of the empire were a common sight in the market streets of Romano-British towns. Wealthy Britons acquired a taste for Roman luxuries, such as expensive wines from Italy. In return, British textiles were sold in Gaul and the Rhineland (the western part of Germany). Silver, lead and tin from British mines were traded throughout the Mediterranean. Trade also helped to spread new ideas. By the year 100, wall paintings and mosaics in many British homes contained images from Roman myths and history.

Roman or British After Death?

Poorer Romans often joined burial clubs to make sure they would be given a proper funeral. Funeral clubs also existed in Roman Britain. The armourers' guild at Bath raised monuments to mark the deaths of its members. Romans usually cremated their dead, but the old Celtic ways persisted. In a 2nd-century Roman cemetery at Brough on Humber, a British corpse was buried in an iron-bound wooden bucket holding two broken sceptres, in the same way as his ancient tribal ancestors.

Roman currency soon began to circulate widely in Britannia. This gold aureus was the most valuable type of coin.

New Towns of the Roman Age

Throughout Britannia, the Romans built well planned towns with grand, stone buildings. The new Roman towns were not just places to live, work and trade, but symbols of imperial wealth and power.

Public Grandeur

The centre of Romano-British towns was the *forum*. This was an open space where the townsfolk met and public ceremonies were held. Here there were statues and Latin inscriptions to the emperor, showing the settlement's loyalty to Rome. On one side of the forum was the *basilica*, where council meetings and law courts were held and the town treasury was kept. The enormous London basilica was 152 m (500 ft) long and 24 m (80 ft) high. At the centre of the larger towns stood a *macellum* or market hall. By 150 CE, the centre of many Romano-British towns would have been instantly recognizable to the Roman traveller.

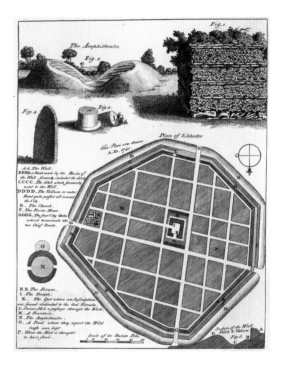

A plan of the Roman town of Silchester shows the forum (meeting place) at the centre, with the amphitheatre outside the town wall.

Playing Games

The Roman taste for bloody gladiatorial combat soon spread to Britain. Amphitheatres seating over 2,500 spectators were built at towns such as Silchester and Caerleon. Romano-British amphitheatres usually had raised earth banks covered with stone and timber tiers, or rows of seating, around a sunken arena. Mosaics of exotic beasts, such as those of tigers

Timeline

50 CE	• Verulamium (St Albans) granted the rank of *municipium* (see box opposite)
71	• Eboracum (York) founded
75	• Settlement established at the Roman base at Iscia Silurum (Caerleon) in Wales
79	• Fortress town of Deva Victris (Chester) founded
120	• Londinium reaches peak population of 60,000 inhabitants
155	• Verulamium destroyed by fire but quickly rebuilt
170	• Londinium has largest basilica north of the Alps
200	• Verulamium covers over 125 acres
380	• Final period in growth of Roman towns

18

found at Woodchester Villa, suggest that these animals were slaughtered in British arenas. After learning Latin, the British elite could also enjoy classical drama. By 60 CE, Colchester had a theatre used for drama as well as for religious ceremonies. No evidence has yet been found of a permanent circus for chariot-racing in Britain, but several mosaics tell us that the Romano-British certainly knew about this exciting Roman sport.

Keeping Clean and Healthy

The Romans believed that cleanliness was very important, so public baths were built in many larger towns such as Exeter and York. The impressive bath-house remains at Wroxeter and Leicester show that vast sums of money were spent on building baths, which were open to everybody. The spa town of Aqua Sulis (Bath) even became a popular centre for pilgrims because its water was believed to have healing powers. Fresh water for the baths was supplied by a network of open stone channels cut into the landscape. At York, an underground grid of stone-lined sewers disposed of the dirty water.

The bath-house was a centre for social and physical activity in Roman Britain. Many bath-houses, such as those at Leicester and Bath (pictured), have survived to the present day.

Town Types

There were four main types of town in Roman Britain. They are shown here with the most important first:

- ◆ *colonia* - a town settled by retired army veterans, for example the city of Lincoln
- ◆ *municipium* - a town whose inhabitants enjoyed the legal status of Roman citizenship, for example St Albans
- ◆ *civitas* - a town that acted as a regional and administrative capital, for example Dorchester
- ◆ *vicus* - a small, temporary settlement close to a Roman army fort that catered for the needs of the troops, for example York, which started as a *vicus* but developed into a *colonia*

The Roman Impact

The Romans had a big impact on the way Britain looked. They built roads, towns and country villas that were the same as those in the rest of their empire.

Roman Roads

Across Britain, Roman surveyors laid out new roads, making sure that they followed the straightest route, the fastest way to get troops and goods from one place to another. Army engineers built the roads with a hard surface and a camber (slope) to allow the rain to drain away quickly. Britannia was soon crisscrossed by a fine network of roads such as Watling Street, which ran from Dover to Wroxeter, and Fosse Way, which linked Exeter to Lincoln.

Roman London

Many of the roads in Britain led to its wealthiest city – Londinium. Camulodunum was the first capital of Roman Britain, but by 100 CE the governor had moved to London. A city of fine stone buildings on the north bank of the River Thames, London had over 60,000 inhabitants. Emperor Hadrian was highly impressed by its amphitheatre, temples and baths when he visited in 122. In 200, the Romans built a high wall around three sides of the city. When Saxon raiders sailed up the Thames, a fourth riverside wall was quickly added. In 205, Britannia was split in two: London remained capital of Lower Britain, while York became capital of Upper Britain.

Roman roads are still visible in many parts of Britain, cutting across the landscape in long, straight lines.

The Countryside

In southern Britain the land was often divided up into large estates, or parcels of land, owned by wealthy families. The centre of the estate was the villa, a large comfortable house surrounded by a wall and useful outbuildings such as larders, baths and a furnace that pumped hot air under the floors of the villa in winter. There were also buildings where the estate's slaves lived. Most villas in Roman Britain had a ground floor built of stone and marble, and an upper timber storey. The inner walls were richly decorated with colourful paintings on plaster, while the floors of the most important rooms were covered in mosaic designs made of small *tesserae* (tiles) of marble.

At Chedworth Roman villa in Gloucestershire, the underfloor heating system can be seen beneath the mosaic tiles in the bath-house.

The Old Ways of Life

In the hilly lands of the West Country, North Wales, the Pennines and Caledonia there were fewer Roman towns and few villas. Here most of the settlements remained more tribal and Celtic in nature. The people used fine Roman objects such as glass, porcelain and jewellery, as many treasure hoards prove, but Latin was heard less often in these places. The main signs of the Roman presence in upland Britain were the distant towers and forts of the legions.

The New Cult of Christ

Members of an outlawed cult, the first Christians in Britain worshipped in secret. In 260, Christianity was permitted as an official religion and a church organization began to emerge.

The distinctive Chi-Rho symbol (seen on the large and small triangular items below) was made up of the first two letters of the word 'Christ' in Greek. It was engraved on many artefacts of 3rd and 4th-century Britain.

Cryptic Clues

For a long time, Christianity was a forbidden faith. The earliest British Christian inscription is a 2nd-century word square found in Manchester. Its letters spell words that the Christians used in their prayers, such as *paternoster, alpha* and *omega.* Fifteen objects in a treasure hoard found at Peterborough also bear the first two letters of Christ's name in Greek.

Villa Christians

Christianity reached Britain through the larger ports, especially London. The first believers were probably humble folk, but the new faith soon had members from the highest ranks of Romano-British society. The grand 4th-century villa at Lullingstone in Kent contained a private Christian chapel, richly decorated with images of believers with arms outstretched in prayer. These images prove that by 300 CE Christianity was common in country areas as well as in the towns, and was a faith for rich and poor.

The First British Saints

The first British martyr was Alban of Verulamium, a Roman soldier executed for helping a persecuted Christian. The Welsh martyrs Aaron and Julius were put to death at Caerleon in 150 CE, but little else is known about them. St Ninian, the apostle of the Picts, is also a mysterious character. A Briton who studied in Rome, he travelled to Pictland and built a church in Galloway in 397.

A Christian Land

We do not know how many people were Christian in Roman Britain. Most of the 5,000 burials in a late Roman cemetery at Poundbury in Dorset were laid out in the Christian way, facing east to west and without grave goods. This tells us that there was a large community of believers there by 275 CE. As the Church grew in numbers, it needed more priests and leaders. Bishops from London, York and Colchester travelled to important church meetings in Gaul in 314 and in Asia Minor in 325.

Pagan Survivors

Christianity became the favoured religion of the Roman Empire in 313. Church leaders quickly set about suppressing other beliefs. All five Mithraic temples found in Britain show signs that they were destroyed by Christians. Nevertheless, there were still pagan places in Britain. The Jupiter column at Cirencester was restored in 360, and a pagan temple was still operating at Maiden Castle in Dorset until 400. The reason for the long survival of paganism was probably because the island of Britain was far away from Rome, where emperors and church leaders were keen to wipe out old beliefs.

This mosaic, from a Roman villa at Hinton St Mary in Dorset, dates from the 4th century and appears to show a portrait of Christ as its central image.

Threats to the Roman Peace

For more than 350 years, southern Britain was a prosperous and secure part of the Roman Empire. After 180 CE, however, the Romano-British increasingly felt that their way of life and safety were under threat.

The Threat From the North

In the late 2nd century, the 'Pictish' tribes of Caledonia began to threaten Britannia. After the death of the strong Emperor Marcus Aurelius in 180, Caledonian warbands raided far to the south. The Romans abandoned their important legionary camp at Trimontium near Melrose soon after. In 207 the Caledonians attacked again. This time Emperor Septimius Severus took charge, gathering an army of 20,000 troops at York. Despite marching into the far north in 209–10, Severus failed to defeat the tribes in battle and Rome lost control of southern Scotland. For the rest of the Roman period, the frontier between Caledonia and Britannia lay along Hadrian's Wall.

The Threat From the Legions

Three legions were needed to protect Roman Britain, but a force of that size was a powerful tool in the hands of an ambitious governor. In 194–6 CE, Clodius Albinus used his command of the legions in Britain to try to make himself emperor. In 210, the Roman government split Britain into two separate parts, in an attempt to make sure that one governor and his army would usually stay loyal to Rome.

After the strong government of Emperor Marcus Aurelius, Britain shared in the turmoil and misery that descended upon the empire in the middle of the 3rd century.

24

The Threat From the Sea

From 280 onwards, Germanic sea-raiders such as the Angles, Saxons and Jutes began to attack the eastern coast of Britannia. In the west, the Irish were also a growing menace. To meet the Saxon threat, the Romans built ten large forts from Portchester in Hampshire to Brancaster in Norfolk. These were garrisoned with fast, heavy cavalry who policed the coast. With walls up to 9 m (30 ft) high and 4.5 m (15 ft) thick, the massive fortifications of the 'Saxon Shore' stopped Germanic raiders from sailing up the rivers of eastern Britain. Nevertheless, most towns in Roman Britain had also built walls by 300.

Emperor Septimius Severus tried to defeat the troublesome tribes of Caledonia. He failed to do so, and in 211 fell ill and died at York.

Carausius, Emperor of Britain

An able soldier of humble birth, Carausius was commander of the Roman fleet in Gaul. Unfairly sentenced to death in 286, he escaped and sailed to Britain and took the title of emperor. An effective ruler, he controlled Britain and northern Gaul for seven years until his assassination in 293. His successor, Allectus, fell in battle near Silchester in 296. The victor Constantius divided Britain into four regions and made sure that their governors could not use the legions against Rome. Constantius made York his imperial headquarters, and strengthened British defences against the growing threat from the Welsh, the Brigantes and the Picts of the north.

Timeline

180 CE	• Beginning of Pictish raids into northern Britannia
208-210	• Emperor Severus' expedition into Caledonia
210	• Britannia is divided into two imperial regions
280	• Coastal raids by Germanic Saxons
286-293	• Brief 'Empire of Britain' under Carausius
290	• 'Saxon Shore' fortifications built on south and eastern coasts
300	• Most Roman towns fortified by this date
306	• Britannia is divided into four imperial regions

367 CE

The Barbarian Onslaught

*In 300 CE, the towns of Roman Britain had strong
walls and the legions were usually able to defend them.
After 350 however, the Roman forces in Britain were
under attack from all directions.*

The Rise of the Picts

In the 4th century, several emperors tried to deal with the hostile
Picts of Caledonia. Constantius Chlorus marched into Pictland
in 305. His son Constantine also campaigned there in 312. But
a Roman writer complained in 360 that
'the Picts disrupted the peace, raiding
and destroying many places near the
frontier'. Emperor Magnus Maximus
thought he had finally defeated the
Picts in 382, but a few years later the
Roman general Stilicho had to send
legions northwards again to meet this
troublesome enemy.

*In the 4th century, the
Picts began to make more
attacks on Roman
territory, pushing further
and further southwards.*

The Barbarian Conspiracy

In 367, the Picts stormed southwards in
great numbers, while waves of Scotii
from Ireland attacked the western
coasts. Saxons overwhelmed the
Roman defences in the south and east.
Hadrian's Wall was seriously breached,
or perhaps by-passed by tribes that had
mastered the skills of seafaring.
Nectaridus, the Roman officer in
charge of the Saxon Shore, was
defeated and killed. The Roman army
in the north was besieged and captured
near York. Roman Britain was
temporarily defeated. Roman writers
believed that Britain had been the
victim of 'a barbarian conspiracy'.

26

A Year of Chaos

In the chaos that followed, order in Roman Britain collapsed. Slaves took their long-awaited revenge on their masters. Soldiers who had deserted the army rampaged through the countryside in search of booty. The attack upon Brislington villa near Bristol is typical of many. The villa buildings were looted and torched and the inhabitants were slaughtered and thrown down the farm well.

The Theodosian Revival

In 370, the Roman emperor sent Count Theodosius to restore order to Britannia. Theodosius made peace with the 'buffer' tribes of southern Caledonia and built a line of coastal towers and beacons to watch the mouths of the Rivers Tyne, Tees and Humber. Hadrian's Wall was repaired. Theodosius also built forts throughout southern Britain to house the cavalry forces needed to meet an agile enemy. Town walls were stiffened with towers to house *ballistae* and other war machines. These changes allowed Roman Britain to defend itself well into the 5th century.

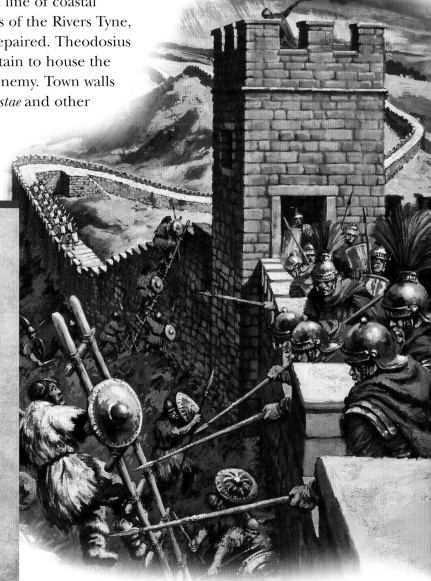

In 367, Hadrian's Wall was breached. Attacks by the Saxons and Franks in the south led to a breakdown of order across Roman Britain.

The Attacotti

The mysterious Attacotti took part in the 367 raids. They probably came from Ireland or from the Scottish Hebrides. St Jerome met some of the Attacotti and noted 'their delight in the taste of human flesh'. Although a warlike people much feared by the Romans, even the Attacotti were absorbed over time into the Roman world. Three Attacotti regiments were part of the Roman army in the late 390s.

The Fall of Roman Britain

Over time, the Roman army and government in Britain were scaled down. One by one, links with the empire faded away. Eventually, the Romano-British found themselves alone.

The Fatal Weakening

In 383, Magnus Maximus sent much of the Roman army in Britain to Gaul because he needed its support in his bid to become emperor. Few of these troops ever returned to Britain, which was no longer properly protected. In the 390s, Irish raiders settled along the coast of Wales. There were now too few legionaries left in Britannia to throw them out.

The Decade of Disaster

In the first decade of the 5th century, barbarian attacks threatened to bring the Roman Empire in Western Europe to its knees. In 401, the Roman general Stilicho was forced to transfer even more men from Britain to stop the Visigoths entering Italy.

Alaric, king of the Visigoth tribe who swept through Europe in the 4th century. Roman legions were forced to leave Britain to try to maintain control on the continent.

Timeline

306-12 CE	• Roman invasions of Pictland
367	• Invasion of Britannia by Picts, Scots and Saxons
370	• Order is restored by Theodosius
383	• Weakening of British legions by Magnus Maximus
400	• Britannia's economic links to rest of the empire are weakened
407	• Remaining Roman legions in Britain are ordered to Gaul
450s	• Germanization of former Roman settlements
450	• Evidence of plague and famine in British towns

Ruins at the site of the Roman city of Viroconium, near Wroxeter in Shropshire.

The last remnants of the Roman army in Britain shipped out of the island in 407, ordered to defend the more important provinces of Gaul and Spain. Traditionally, the year 410 is said to mark the end of Roman Britain. There was, however, no sudden withdrawal of legions on that date. Roman strength in Britain had been seeping away for years.

Economic Decline

Romano-British prosperity quickly came to an end after 400 CE. After that date, no imperial coinage could be spared for distant Britannia. Money became scarce and the demand for expensive goods dried up. Ships carrying produce from Europe arrived less frequently. The quality of British goods also declined badly as the skills to make mosaics, pottery or window-glass faded away. Romanized homes were expensive to maintain. Instead, by the 450s, Germanic settlements of thatched timber huts were springing up around the crumbling Roman towns. A Romanized life continued for some decades, but the public baths and temples fell into disrepair and disuse. Finally, years of plague and famine around 450 drew a line between Britain's prosperous Roman past and its uncertain future.

The Roman Legacy

Three-and-a-half centuries of Roman civilization left a lasting mark on Britain. Grass now grew on the roads the legions had built, but they continued to be used, forming a network of routes that has survived to the present day. Some Roman settlements faded away. Wroxeter (above) never recovered from its burning at the hands of Irish raiders, but most Roman towns continued in use as settlements. The Romans left something more behind. The limits of their power in the north and west reinforced the geography of Britain. The Roman failure to conquer all of Britain meant that, in the future, there would be more than one centre of power on the islands.

Glossary

alpha and **omega** the ancient Greek for 'beginning' and 'end'

archaeological to do with the study of the past through the scientific analysis of remains, such as buildings, artefacts and bones

ballista a Roman war machine, like a giant crossbow (plural: *ballistae*)

barrage the repeated bombardment of an area

beacon a bonfire on a tower lit as a warning signal

bolt the metal arrow fired by a Roman catapult

booty valuable stolen goods

Caledonia the Roman name for northern Scotland

cavalry troops on horseback

classical a word describing anything Roman or ancient Greek

elite the leaders of a community

entrails the inner organs of a human or animal body

garrison troops that are based in a fortress

Gaul the Roman name for France

grave goods important belongings buried alongside a person in a grave

Hibernia the Roman name for Ireland

homage a public display of honour or respect

larder a room used for storing supplies of food and drink

legion a regiment in the Roman army of about 6,000 men

legionaries soldiers in a Roman legion

magistrates officials who carry out the law

martyr a person who dies or is killed because of his or her beliefs

Mithraic describes things, such as temples and artefacts, that are associated with the ancient Persian god, Mithras

mosaic a pattern or picture made from small pieces of coloured tiles

pagan describes a person who holds religious beliefs that are not those of the world's main religions

paternoster the Latin for 'Our Father'

Picts the peoples of northern Scotland

pilgrim a traveller to a place of holiness and/or healing

Romano-British describes the Britons who took up Roman ways of life

sceptre a ceremonial rod or wand

Scotii the Roman name for a tribe from northern Ireland

villa a large, comfortable house surrounded by a wall and outbuildings

Visigoths an eastern people who invaded the Roman Empire around 400 CE

Timeline

55–54 BCE	• First unsuccessful attempts by Romans to invade Britain
43 CE	• Romans invade and conquer much of south-eastern England
60–61 CE	• Boudicca leads the revolt of the Iceni against Roman rule
66–78 CE	• Romans attack and defeat the Druidic tribes of North Wales
79–82 CE	• Tribes of southern Scotland pacified by the legions
84 CE	• Battle of Mons Graupius in northern Scotland
122–7 CE	• Construction of Hadrian's Wall from Tyne to Solway
140 CE	• Construction of Antonine's Wall from Forth to Clyde
205 CE	• Britannia split into two parts – Upper and Lower Britain
209–10 CE	• Emperor Severus fails to conquer the Picts
280 CE	• Southern and eastern coasts of Britannia attacked by Germanic raiders
286–96 CE	• Short-lived 'British Empire' under Carausius and Allectus
367 CE	• Year of 'the barbarian conspiracy'
370 CE	• Restoration of Roman order by Count Theodosius
383–401 CE	• Roman legions in Britain seriously weakened
400 CE	• Last payment of Roman money to Britannia
407 CE	• Last Roman army units sail from Britain

Further Information

Books

Roman Britain, A Historical Map and Guide, Ordnance Survey, 2001

Roman Britain: A Very Short Introduction, Peter Salway, Oxford Paperbacks, 2000

Roman Fort, Margaret Mulvihill, Franklin Watts, 2006

A Roman Journey, Alex Woolf, Wayland, 2004

Look Inside a Roman Villa, Richard Dargie, Hodder Wayland, 2002

Websites

http://www.roman-britain.org/
vast website with maps and guides to all aspects of life in Roman Britain

http://www.bbc.co.uk/history/ancient/romans/
interactive games, virtual 3D tours of Roman British sites and information on many aspects of life in Roman Britain

http://www.brims.co.uk/romans/
fun, introductory website with sections on the Romans in Britain

http://www.bbc.co.uk/scotland/education/
simple interactive fun site about the Romans and the natives of Caledonia

http://www.britannia.com/history/h30.html
timelines, biographies, maps, lists, site guides, information about Roman Britain

http://www.hadrians-wall.org/
portal to a vast range of resources relating to Hadrian's Wall

http://www.grahamthomas.com/history4.html
informative guide to the Romano-British villa at Woodchester near Bath

Index